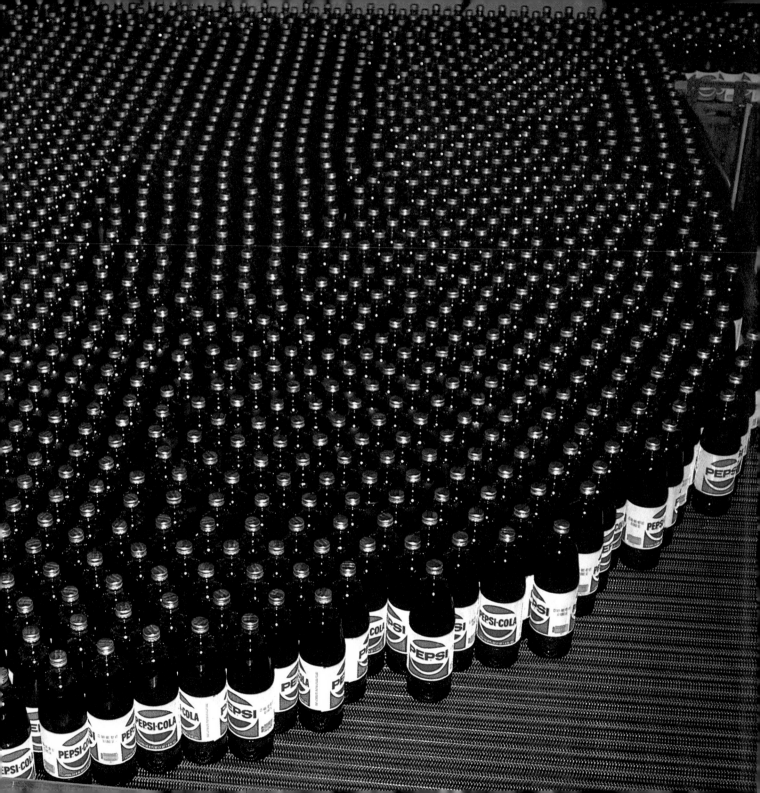

How Does Soda Get Into the Bottle?

Written and Photographed by
OZ CHARLES

Simon and Schuster Books for Young Readers
Published by Simon & Schuster, New York

This book would not be possible without the patience, help, and cooperation of the management and all of the employees of the Pepsi-Cola Bottling Company of New York, Inc., in Long Island City.

The author wishes to thank Sinar Bron, Inc. for the use of their photographic studio.

With special thanks to Pamela D. Pollack, Grace D. Clarke, and Sylvia Frezzolini.

SIMON AND SCHUSTER BOOKS FOR YOUNG READERS is a trademark of Simon & Schuster, Inc.
SIMON & SCHUSTER and colophon are registered trademarks of Simon & Schuster, Inc.

Designed by Sylvia Frezzolini
Manufactured in the United States of America

10 9 8 7 6 5 4 3 2 1

Library of Congress Cataloging-in-Publication Data
Charles, Oz.   How does soda get into the bottle?
Summary: Text and photographs depict all the stages in the manufacture of a soft drink, from syrup to bottled product.   1. Carbonated beverages—Juvenile literature.   [1. Carbonated beverages]
I. Title.   TP630.C518 1988   663'.62   87-11534
ISBN 0-671-63755-X

To Norma,
for all her encouragement and faith

On hot summer days, cold winter nights, and everything in between, millions and millions of people are drinking millions and millions of bottles of soda. With the exception of water, soda is the most popular and widely consumed beverage in America. Have you ever wondered how soda gets into all those bottles?

Soda is made and bottled at the bottling plant. The process begins in the syrup room. In this room are huge steel tanks, which store liquid sugar. Each tank holds 15,000 gallons of sugar. Large steel barrels, or drums, are filled with "syrup concentrate." Syrup concentrate is not sweet. It is a combination of flavor essences, like vanilla extract. Those are the ingredients that give each soda its special flavor.

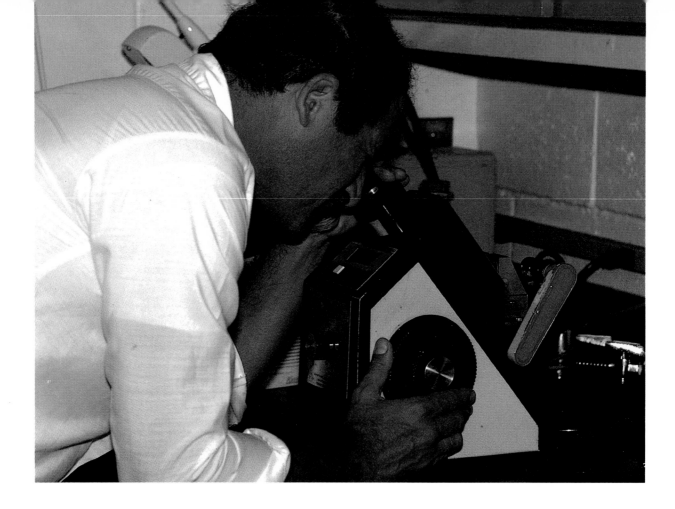

First, water is mixed with liquid sugar to make a "simple syrup." This mixture is then checked for strength—is it too sweet? Or not sweet enough?

The machine that does the testing is called a refractometer. A small amount of syrup is put on a glass prism. Light is passed through the syrup, and the light beam is bent (or refracted), casting a shadow on a scale. By reading the number in the shadow, a technician can see how much sugar is present. (The more sugar, the higher the number.)

The next ingredient is the syrup concentrate (flavor essence). This is suctioned out of its barrels and mixed with the "simple syrup" (water and sugar) in a large mixing tank. After all the mixing is finished, it is called "finished syrup."

This finished syrup is also tested in the refractometer. Does it have the right amount of water? Sugar? The color is checked by a machine called a colorimeter. It is also *tasted* by a technician.

Having passed all the tests, the finished syrup is sent through large pipes to the flow-mix machine, also called the proportioner.

The flow-mix machine has two upper chambers, and each one has holes at the bottom. One holds treated water, the other holds finished syrup.

Water and syrup drip through the holes and into a lower chamber, where they blend together. For each cup of syrup, there are five to seven cups of water, depending upon what kind of soda is being made.

The next stop is a machine called the carbo-cooler. This is where bubbles are put into the soda. The carbo-cooler is filled with carbon dioxide gas. Inside the carbo-cooler are cold coils, like in a refrigerator. This keeps the temperature at about 38 degrees.

The liquid from the flow-mix machine is sprayed into the carbo-cooler, where it absorbs the carbon dioxide gas as it passes through and out of the bottom. Carbo-coolers hold from 30 to 50 gallons of soda at a time.

Meanwhile, thousands of empty bottles are taken out of cartons. A machine called the uncaser pulls them out and puts them onto a conveyor belt. A conveyor belt is a moving platform which brings something from one place to another.

The bottles, which are dry and dusty from sitting in cardboard boxes, are sprayed with water to keep them from sticking together as they are moved along the conveyor belt to the rinser.

The bottles are moved single file onto the rinser to be cleaned. The rinser turns them upside down. They are rinsed, inside and out, and allowed to drip-dry.

Now the bottles are ready to be filled. They move along the conveyor belt until they reach the filler.

The filler looks like a merry-go-round. The bottles are shifted onto this moving carousel by big wheels called stars, and each one is held in place by stirrups. A metal tube is inserted into each bottle, and soda is dropped in.

When bottles are filled, they are shifted off the carousel by another star onto another conveyor belt, and are replaced with more empty bottles.

The next step is the capper, a machine that puts caps onto filled bottles. Above the capper is the hopper. The hopper is filled with hundreds of caps which come down a chute, one by one, onto the bottles as they go into the capper.

Each cap is put on a bottle by two pairs of metal wheels. One pair presses the cap very tightly to fit around the grooved neck of the bottle. The other pair tucks the edges under, to make it "tamper resistant." This way you can always tell if a bottle has been opened or not.

The filled, capped bottles are sent along the conveyor belt to the warmer. The soda, which is still quite cold from having been in the carbo-cooler, needs to be warmed up to room temperature. Have you ever noticed that when you pour a cold glass of soda on a hot day, the outside of your glass gets wet? Well, the same thing happens here. The difference between the coldness of the soda and the warmness of the air makes the bottles wet and slippery. They have to be warm and dry, so that they can be packed into cardboard cartons.

The warmer sprays the bottles with warm water. The warm water on the bottles makes the soda warm very quickly. After they leave the warmer the warm bottles dry very quickly.

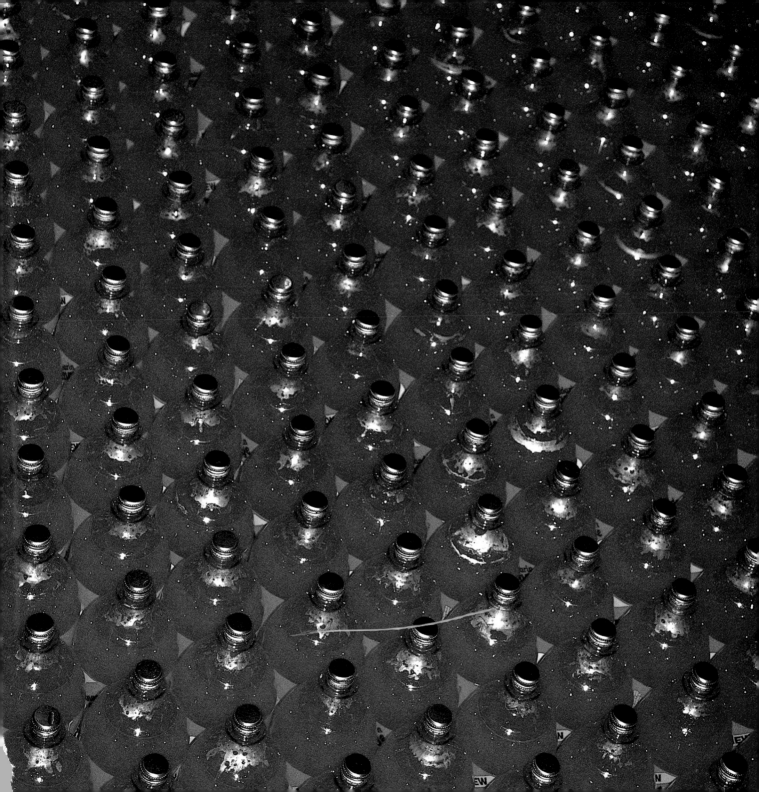

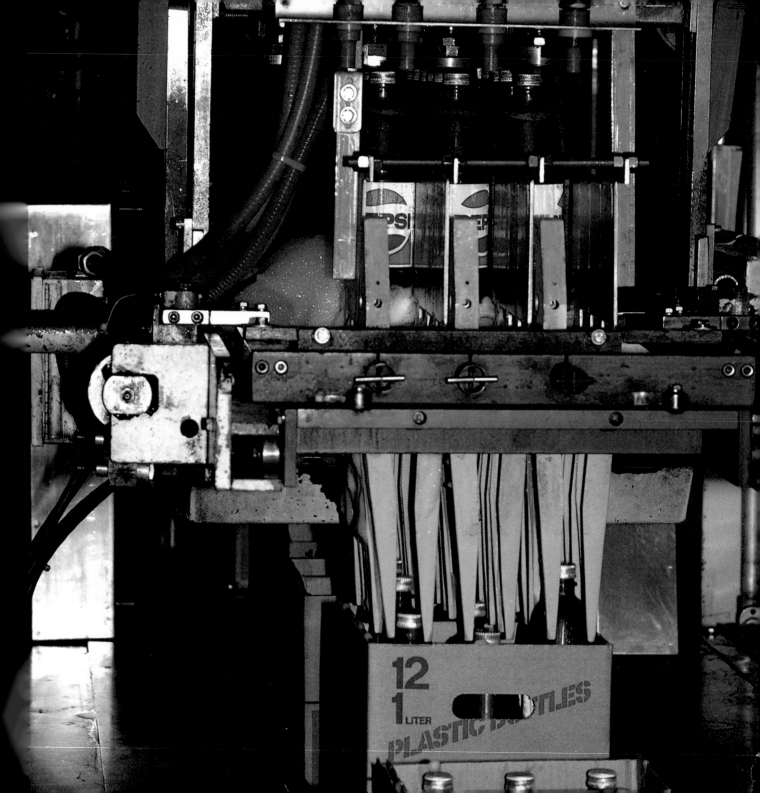

The bottles are moved to the packer, which puts them into empty cartons. When a carton is filled, it is automatically closed and glued by the packer. The carton moves along the conveyor belt until it reaches a machine called a palletizer.

The palletizer stacks the cartons onto wooden platforms (pallets). A forklift truck then lifts each pallet and takes them to the shipping area. The cartons of soda are loaded onto trucks and delivered to supermarkets and grocery store shelves.

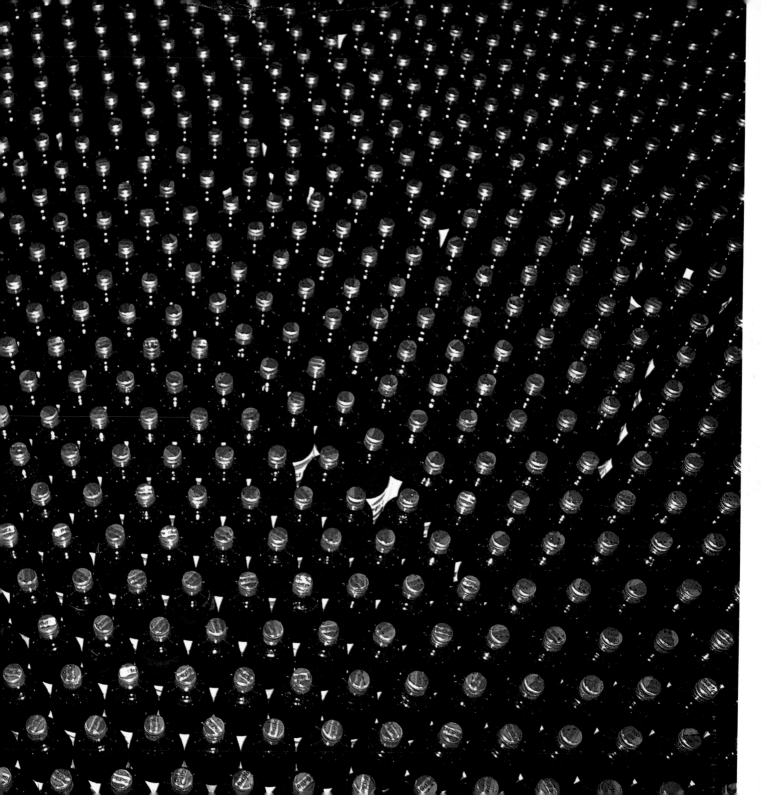